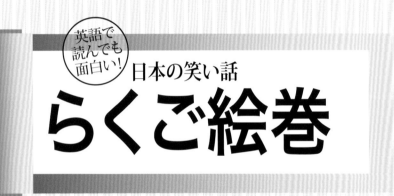

英語で読んでも面白い！ 日本の笑い話

らくご絵巻

Laugh along in English! traditional japanese comic storytelling

A RAKUGO PICTURE BOOK

はじめに

古典落語は不思議なアートです。

師匠から弟子へ、言葉だけで伝えられて、百年も二百年も、そのストーリーが残ります。

そして、その歴史の最先端にいる演者が、自分なりのアレンジをして、また、次の世に送ります。

その物語の世界は、聴く人の想像力の中で広がり、聴く人ひとりひとり、自分だけのビジュアル世界に浸れるのです。

自分以外の人は、どんな世界を想像しているのだろう?

そんな興味に誘惑されて、古典落語をビジュアル化してみました。

絵本では、ときどき見かけますが、これは、おとなも楽しめる絵巻。

落語通の皆さんには、「そうなんだ、こんな世界だ！」「いや、この人物はちょっと

違うな」と、いろいろツッコミを入れながらページをめくっていただいて、

落語初心者の皆さんには、純粋に物語を楽しんでいただいて、

後日、確認のために寄席に出向いていただければ、幸いです。

今回、チョイスした二題、テーマは「ミラクルでハッピー！」。

思いがけない不思議なことで、普通の人が幸運を摑むお話を選びました。

このごろ多くなってきた、日本文化のお好きな海外の方にも楽しんでいただけるよう、

英文も付けました。

後世に落語の文化を伝える、ひとつのステップになれば幸いです。

もりた はじめ

3

目次

CONTENTS

日本の笑い話

らくご絵巻 その一

ぞろぞろ

ZOROZORO

古いお話でございます。

昔は、武家屋敷や大きな商家の庭の隅には、

必ずお稲荷様をお祀りしていたようで。

年月を経て、家屋敷が無くなり、野原になっても、

お稲荷様だけはそのまま残ってしまったりいたします。

This is a story from long, long ago.

In the old days, one could find a shrine to the harvest god Inari-sama on the grounds of any large estate owned by samurai or wealthy merchants.

As time passed and fortunes changed, many of these houses fell into ruin and vanished, but often the Inari shrines would remain, standing alone in empty fields.

ここにございますのは、浅草の近郊でございます。

太郎稲荷という、小さな森を背負ったお稲荷様で、あたりは静かな田園風景で

ございます。

近くには、荒物（あらもの）や駄菓子（だがし）、小間物（こまもの）類も扱う茶店が一軒。それでも以前は、

少し参詣（さんけい）の人もいたのですが、ほかに通行に便利な道でも

できたのでしょうか、今はもう、めったに訪れる人もおりません。

茶店のじいさんは、きょうも床几（しょうぎ）でお茶を飲みながら、ばあさんと話をしています。

10

Here, in one such field on the outskirts of Asakusa,

with the backdrop of a shady grove, stands a shrine known as Tarō Inari.

All around is quiet countryside. But a short distance up the dirt road from the

shrine is a tea house selling sweets and a few miscellaneous sundries.

Isolated though the spot is, people used to pass by fairly often on their way to

pray at Tarō Inari. Now, however, perhaps because of a convenient new road

that bypasses the area, visitors are extremely rare.

The old man who runs the tea house sits on a stool sipping tea and talking to his

wife.

11

「なあ、ばあさん。きょうもいい天気じゃが、

お参りは無いなあ。昔は、ここでもよう売れた。

旅人が通る道じゃったでなあ。茶は飲むし、菓子も喰う。

脚絆や菅笠や、草鞋や懐紙なんぞも、

よく売れたもんじゃ。

今ではどうじゃ。お稲荷さんも荒れ果ててのう」

「またまた、おじいさん。昔の話ばっかり。

愚痴を言うと、お稲荷様に申し訳がありませんよ。

おじいさんが、もうちょっと

朝早く起きて、境内を掃除して、

お稲荷様に、しっかりお願い

してみたらどうです」

12

"Well, old girl, it's another beautiful day, and once again no one's visiting the shrine. Remember how it used to be? We always did good business, on account of travelers having to use this old road. They'd stop and drink some tea. They'd eat some sweets. Sometimes they'd buy leggings, or bamboo hats or straw sandals. And now? Nothing. Even the shrine down the road is looking shabby and abandoned."

"There you go again, talking about days gone by. All your grumbling is disrespectful to Tarō Inari. Why don't you get up a little earlier each morning, sweep the shrine grounds, and pray to Inari-sama for help?"

13

それもそうじゃな、と、このじいさん、

一念発起いたしまして、翌日から早起きで、

お稲荷様をきれいに掃除をいたします。

Seeing the merit of his wife's suggestion, the old man resolves to do exactly that. Each morning from then on, he rises early and goes to the shrine to clean up and pray.

「お稲荷様、なにとぞ、もうちょっとでよろしいので、

通行の旅人がふえまして、茶店が繁盛^{はんじょう}しますように・・・」

と、一心に拝みます。

"O Inari-sama, please send a few travelers this way, to make our tea house a little more prosperous."

そんな日が続きまして、七日目のことでございます。

いつものように、おじいさんがお稲荷様を拝み、

帰ろうとすると、ポツポツと、雨でございます。

Day after day he delivers this heartfelt prayer. Then, on the seventh day, something happens.

The old man is returning from the shrine that morning, when raindrops start to fall: *Plip, plop. Plop, plip, plip.*

大急ぎで茶店へ戻りますと、ザッと本降り。

道がすっかり、ぬかるんでおります。

「ごめんよ！」

勢いよくひとりの旅人が走り込んでまいります。

He hurries home and ducks inside just as it really begins

to pour: *SHAAAAA!*

The dirt path outside is soon a muddy, slippery mess. And now a rare passing

traveler dashes into the shop.

"Sorry to burst in like this!"

「おー、降られちゃったよ。じいさん済ま

ねえ。ワラジ、くんな。この道じゃ、歩けねえ」

「へいへい。ワラジなんぞは、

あまり売れませんのでな、ここに一足、

ホコリをかぶったものが吊ってございます

が、これでよろしゅうございますなら」

「いいとも。ホコリなんざ、はたけば

いいのさ。ほい、六文」

旅人は銭を置いて出て行きます。

この日は、雨のせいですか、旅人が帰り

ますと、また次のお客がまいります。

"Got caught in the rain! I need some straw sandals, old fellow. Can't walk through this mud without 'em."

"Yes, sir. We don't sell many sandals, so all we have is the one pair hanging in the corner here, all covered with dust. If these will do ..."

"They'll be fine. Slap the soles together like this, and goodbye dust. Here you go: six *mon*."

The traveler hands the coins over and exits in his new sandals.

It must have something to do with the rain: no sooner has he left than another customer appears.

23

「おじいさん、ワラジを一足

いただきたいのだが・・・」

「あいにく、ついさっき一足あったものが売

れてしまいまして。あい済まぬことで」

「うーん。そこに吊ってあるのは、

売らんのかな?」

「え? あ? あれ? ありましたな。歳を

とると見落としましてな」

天井からワラジを引き抜いて、渡します。

24

"I need a pair of sandals!"

"I'm so sorry, sir. We just sold our only pair."

"Huh? You mean the pair hanging right there isn't for sale?"

"The … Oh! Well, what do you know? I overlooked that pair somehow. Must be getting old."

He pulls the sandals down and hands them over in exchange for six more *mon*.

25

「亭主、ワラジを一足、所望じゃ」

こんどはお武家でございます。

「あいにく、ワラジは・・・」

「そこに吊ってあるではないか」

「あれれれれ?」

"Shopkeeper!" This time it's a passing samurai.

"I require a pair of straw sandals."

"Unfortunately, we have no—"

"What's that hanging right there?"

"Who wuh wah?"

27

じいさんは、わけがわからず、吊ってあるワラジを引っ張りますと、

天井の隅から、新しいワラジが、ぞろぞろ！　と一足出てまいります。

また引っ張ると、ぞろぞろ。それを引っ張ると、また、ぞろぞろ。

The old man has no idea how or why, but each time he pulls a pair of sandals

down from the ceiling—*zorozoro*—a new pair appears to

take its place.

Pull that pair down and—*zorozoro*—here's another one.

Grab it and pull and, sure enough: *zorozoro*!

このできごとが近郷近在（きんごうきんざい）で評判になりまして、

太郎稲荷のご利益（りやく）にあやかりたい。

ぞろぞろ出てくるワラジを見たい。

おじいさんの茶店は、いっぱいのお客様で、大繁盛。

お稲荷様も、遠くからお参りもあり、大賑（にぎ）わいでございます。

News of this miracle spreads throughout the surrounding countryside.

Everyone hopes to receive a similar blessing from Tarō Inari—or at least to

watch the sandals magically appear, *zorozoro*, one pair after another.

The old couple's tea house is packed each day and prospering like never before.

The shrine too is now thriving, with crowds coming from near and far to

worship.

この話を聞きましたのが、隣町の床屋の親方です。

「そうか、うちもこの頃、お客がさっぱり。

ひとつ、わしもお稲荷様へお願いしてみようか?」

It's not long before a barber in a nearby town gets wind of the story.

"Hmm. I haven't had any customers either lately. Maybe I ought to go ask for a

blessing myself."

この床屋、茶店のおじいさんにあやかりまして、

自分もきっちり、毎朝拝みにまいります。

「どうか私にも、茶店のワラジのようなご利益をくださいませ」

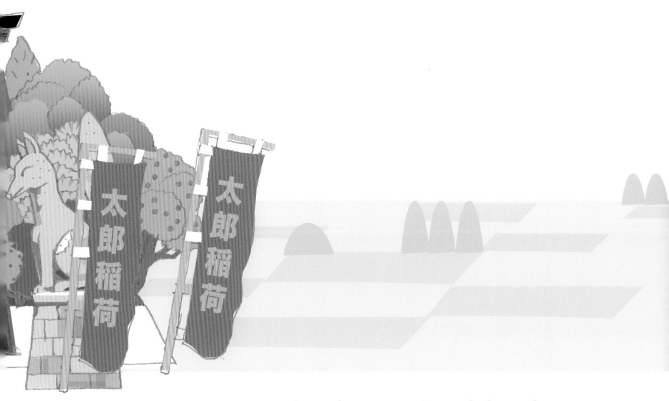

Following the old man's example, the barber starts rising each day at dawn to pray at Tarō Inari.

"O Inari-sama, please bless my barber shop, just like you did with those tea-house sandals."

で、やはり、七日目のことでございます。

「ああ、きょうで七日目だ、お客がたくさんくるかしらん?」

と、店へ帰りますと、三人もお客が待っています。

A week goes by. And then ...

"So, this is the seventh day! Maybe business will start to pick up now."

The barber hurries back from the shrine that morning to find not one, not two,

but three customers waiting for him. The first in line steps forward.

「親方、これから上方へ行くんだよ。

ひげ当たってくんな。急ぎだよ」

なんとすごい！　お稲荷様のご利益は

テキメン！　親方は大喜びです。

42

"I'm leaving for the capital and need my beard shaved right away!"

"Yes, sir!"

The barber is overjoyed. Hallelujah! Behold the timely blessings of Inari-sama!

早速、最初のお客に腰かけてもらい、顔を湯で湿して、

カミソリで、スーとひげを剃りますと・・・

He seats the customer, moistens his face with hot water, and begins removing

his beard.

The razor is sharp and slices smoothly through the whiskers.

そのあとから、新しいひげが・・・

ぞろぞろ。

And as each hair drops, a new one sprouts up to replace it:

ZOROZORO!

ぞろぞろ・オチのあとさき

このオチ、笑いのツボは、ご利益を授ける（さず）お稲荷さんの勘違い（かんちが）。

というところですかね。

ワラジをひとつ取ると次が出てくるというミラクルは、まあ、いいでしょう。急に莫大（ばくだい）な金銀を授けても、老夫婦には遣い道も無いし、物騒（ぶっそう）ですしね。仕入れなくても、売れて売れて、どんどん売れるワラジ。いくら売れても、あんまり大きな金額にはなりませんが、このぐらいがちょうどいい。商売が忙しいということは、老夫婦には足腰の運動にもなるし、生き甲斐（がい）にもなる。どこか近くの温泉へ二人で、半年に一度ぐらいは行かせてあげたいもんだ。お稲荷さんは、そう考えたのでしょう。なかなか思慮深い、いいお稲荷さんです。元来、お稲荷さんは、稲の豊作をつかさどる神様ですから、ぞろぞろと、成長させるのは得意技なのかも知れません。

と、まあ、ここまではいいのですが、床屋の親父（おやじ）が出てきたので、ちょっと、お稲荷さ

んも混乱したんですな。「はて？　今度は、何を授ければ喜ぶんだろう？」お稲荷さんのアタマには、あのうれしそうな茶店のじいさんの顔が目に浮かびます。じいさんに幸せを与えて、床屋には知らん顔もできない、ここらあたりは、大変義理堅いお稲荷さんでもあります。ワラジの成功を何とか生かしたい。床屋は、何がぞろぞろ出てくると喜ぶのであろうか？　そうか！　床屋は髪の毛やひげが生えていると商売になるんだ！　と、考えるのですが、このへんが、さすがお稲荷さん、少し浮世ばなれしているのです。そんな具合で、オチでは大変なことになるのですが、この話、このあとどうなるのか心配ですね。剃ってもぞろぞろ！　また剃ってもぞろぞろ！　だと、お客は永久に帰れません。

落語に教訓はありませんが、もし、あるとすれば、神頼みも人まねではなく、オリジナリティを大切にせよ。ということでしょうか？　皆様も人まねには、お気をつけください。

49

A WORD ON "ZOROZORO"

The punch line (or *ochi*) of this story is the single word that also serves as the title. *Zorozoro* is a phenomime, a word that acts much like onomato-poeia but evokes movement rather than sound. The Japanese language is blessed with dozens of these colorful and often untranslatable words.

Other examples of phenomimes include *guruguru*, *batabata*, and *choko-choko*, each of which describes a distinct type of motion or action. "Zoro-zoro" evokes rapid growth or proliferation, making it an apt descriptor for blessings bestowed by a harvest god.

日本の笑い話

らくご絵巻 その二

ぬけ雀

POP-OUT SPARROWS

古いお話でございます。

昔は、旅は歩いてしたものでございまして。そのための道路がちゃんと作られて

いたそうでございますな。お江戸日本橋を起点にいたしまして、京・大阪へまいり

ますのは東海道五十三次と申しまして、五十三か所の宿場町がございます。この

お話は、東海道の大きな宿場町のひとつ、小田原宿が舞台でございます。

日本橋

品川

川崎

神奈川

保土ヶ谷

In the old days, most people traveled on foot, but a person of wealth might ride in a *kago*. This was a curtained platform suspended from a pole and borne by a pair of laborers known as *kago-kaki*. *Kago-kaki* plied their trade up and down early highways like the Tokaido Road, which began at Nihombashi in old Edo and stretched all the way to Kyoto and Osaka. The famous "Fifty-three Stations of the Tokaido" were towns along the way featuring inns for travelers. Our story takes place in Odawara, one of the larger inn towns.

藤沢

平塚

大磯

小田原

宿場町の夕暮れは大変賑やかでございます。

「えー、お泊まりはいかがですか?」「えー、眺めのいいお部屋が空いております」

いい宿へ泊まろうと物色する旅人、うちへ泊めようと客引きをする宿屋の番頭

などで、道はごった返しております。

そんな中にひとり、まだ若い紋付姿の旅人が、歩いております。

An inn town is a lively, bustling place of an early evening.

"Welcome! Looking for a nice place to stay?"

"Halloa! We're offering a room with a splendid view!"

The streets are jammed with travelers seeking quality lodgings and inn-clerks

seeking customers.

Through the crowd strolls a lone young traveler.

この人には宿屋の番頭が声を掛けないのですな。

それもそのはず、その身なりの汚いこと。黒紋付といっても、

すっかり染めの黒地がはげて、茶色紋付になってございます。

袴_{はかま}もよれよれ。帯もところどころ、ほつれていようという。

足は素足_{すあし}に藁草履_{わらぞうり}。顔立ちは幾分立派なのですが、

かなり、うす汚れております。誰にも声を掛けられないまま、

宿場はずれまで来てしまうと、そこに相模屋_{さがみや}という小さな

旅籠_{はたご}が一軒、主の善兵衛_{ぜんべえ}が、表で客引きをしております。

58

None of the inn-clerks call out to him, however, for one very obvious reason: his remarkably disheveled appearance. Though his kimono is a formal one, complete with family crest, it's a ratty-looking thing. The black silk has faded to a stained, rusty brown; the obi sash is wrinkled and threadbare; and he wears straw sandals with no stockings. The young man's features are not unattractive, but his face is dirty.

He walks all the way to the outskirts of town without anyone calling to out him. But here he meets up with the innkeeper Zembei. Zembei is standing in front of the inn he keeps, the Sagami-ya.

「えーお泊まりはいかがですか?」

「わしか?」

「さようでございます。よろしければお泊まりを」

「泊まってもよいが、ちと長逗流<ruby>長逗流<rt>ながとうりゅう</rt></ruby>になるかも知れぬ。

わしは一日に酒を三升飲むが、はじめに二、三十両<ruby>両<rt>りょう</rt></ruby>でも

預けておいたほうがよいか?」

「いえいえ、どなた様に限らずお勘定<ruby>勘定<rt>かんじょう</rt></ruby>はお発ち<ruby>発<rt>た</rt></ruby>の時で

結構でございます。私どもは私と女房<ruby>女房<rt>にょうぼう</rt></ruby>と、少しの奉公人<ruby>奉公人<rt>ほうこうにん</rt></ruby>

だけでやっております小さな旅籠ですが、

親切を第一に商い<ruby>商<rt>あきな</rt></ruby>をしております」

「そうか。気に入った、それでは泊めてもらおう」

60

"Hi there! Need a place to stay?"

"Who, me?"

"Yes, sir! How about staying with us?"

"Well, I suppose I could do that, but it might be a rather lengthy stay. And I will require three bottles of sake daily. I suppose it would be best if I handed over twenty or thirty *ryō* of gold up front?"

"That won't be necessary, sir. We're happy to let all our guests settle their bill on departure. I say 'we,' but it's just me and my wife running this little inn, don't you know, and, well, our number one policy is friendliness."

"Is that so? Most agreeable. Lead the way."

61

二階の座敷に入ります。

「風呂はよい。飯にしてくれ。酒を一升。冷やでよいぞ」

別に酒の肴を誂えるでもなく、膳の上のお菜で、ぺろりと一升をたいらげてしまいます。

The young traveler is shown to a room upstairs.

"Never mind the bath. Bring my dinner. One bottle of sake. No need to heat it."

He doesn't ask for any snacks to complement his sake but makes short work of

the half-gallon bottle.

明くる朝、早く起きまして、朝飯の時にまた一升。これも何事もなく飲んで、小さな

風呂敷包みをひとつだけ持って表へ出てしまいます。昼過ぎには帰ってまいりま
^(ふろしきづつ)

して、昼飯。昼からまた一升。ごろんと横になったかと思うと、夕飯ではまた一升。

明けますと、朝飯で一升、表へ出る。

「善兵衛、小田原は良いところだな。気に入った」

というわけで、五日間ほど、そんな日が続きます。

Arising early the next morning, he orders another bottle with breakfast. He downs this casually enough, wraps a few things in a small bundle, and strolls outside. Shortly after noon he returns and has lunch, along with another bottle. He then lies down for a while, and pretty soon it's time for dinner and one more bottle. Sleep, breakfast, another bottle, stroll outside ...

"You know, Zembei, I've become quite fond of Odawara.

What a delightful place!"

And so it goes for some five days and nights.

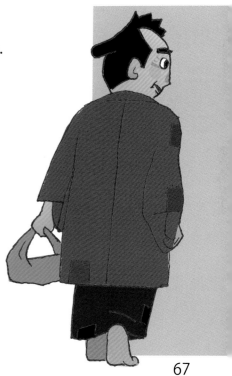

「ちょいと、お前さん。なんかおかしくないかい?」

「何が?」

「二階の客だよ。毎日毎日、よくあれだけお酒が飲めるね、まったく。

それに、何さ、あの汚いきもの。ちょいとって引っ張ればビリーと破れそうだよ。

ひょろっとつまずくと、ピーと裂けそう。ちょいビリのひょろっピーだよ。

ひょっとしてまた一文無しじゃないの?」

「そんなことねえよ。最初に二、三十両でも預けておこうかとおっしゃったんだ」

「そんなら、これまでのお酒代だけでも、

と言って貰っておいでよ。わたしゃ心配だよ。

お前さんは人が好いんだから」

"Listen, old man. Something fishy is going on, don't you think?"

"With what?"

"The guest upstairs. The way that man drinks each day! And what about that filthy old kimono of his? If he slips he'll rip it, and if he trips he'll strip it. Slippety rippety trippety strippety—that's him. Are you sure he's not just another wandering pauper?"

"Ridiculous. The first thing he did was ask me if he should deposit thirty *ryō* ."

"Then at least go ask him to pay for all the sake he's drunk so far. I'm worried. You're such an easy mark!"

かみさんに尻を叩かれまして、善兵衛さん、二階へあがってまいります。

"With his wife lighting a fire beneath him, Zembei makes his way upstairs.

「お客様、よろしゅうございますか」

「おお善兵衛か。よいぞ。なんだ?」

「あのー、実は、誠に申しあげにくいんですけれども、

酒屋の払いが滞っておりまして、

お宿代は、申しあげました通りお発ちの時でよろしいので、酒代だけを入れてい

ただくわけにはまいりませんでしょうか?」

「なるほど。如何ほどになるのじゃ」

「へい。二両二分になります」

「なに? あれだけの酒を飲んで、たったの二両二分か。安いのう」

「へい。ありがとうございます」

"May I come in, sir?"

"Zembei! Of course. What's on your mind?"

"Well, er, the truth is, sir, well, I don't like saying this, but, you see, our bill with the sake merchant is long overdue, and although it's customary here to pay for the room on departure, as I mentioned before, well, I wonder if I might not trouble you to cover just the cost of the sake you've consumed thus far."

"I see. And how much does it come to?"

"Thank you, sir. Two and a half *ryō*."

"That's it? All that sake for just two and a half *ryō*? So cheap!"

"Thank you, sir."

73

「払ってやりたいのは山々なのだが、金は無いのだ。一文も無い」

「え？　しかし、最初に二、三十両でも預けておいたらよかろうかと…」

「預けておいたらいいだろうなあと思ったまでじゃ。無い。許せ」

「そんな殺生（せっしょう）な、あなた。いけませんよ。どうするんです」

「と言われても、無いものは無い。わしが、今度、江戸から帰ってくるまで待て」

「困りますよ。あなた。あなたは一体、お仕事は何なんです？」

「わしは、絵師（えし）だ。まだ修業の身じゃが。そうだ、約束に、何か描いておこう」

「描いておこうったって…あなた、弱っちゃったなあ」

"I'd like to pay you right this minute, in fact. Sadly, however, I have no money."

"Sir?"

 "Not a copper *mon* to my name."

"What? But ... but you asked me that first day if you should deposit twenty or thirty *ryō*!"

"All I said was that I supposed it would be best if I could do that. Didn't mean I could do it. Sorry."

"Outrageous! Listen, you. You can't get away with this. You must do something!"

"Easy for you to say, Zembei, but I can't give you what I haven't got.

You'll have to wait till I return from Edo."

"Unacceptable. Look here. What kind of work

do you do, exactly?"

"I'm an *e-kaki*, a picture-painter. Still just

learning my art, mind you, but ... That's it! I'll

paint you something and leave it as collateral."

"Paint me something? Good heavens.

Listen, mister ..."

75

「あれは、なんだ、向こうの部屋にある」

「ああ、あれは衝立ですよ。あんたみたいな一文無しが泊まってね。仕事が表具師だって言うから、あれを宿代がわりに張らせたんですよ。うちはよく一文無しが泊まるね」

76

"Say! What's that over there in the next room?"

"What, the partition screen? Yes, let me tell you about that. We had a no-account pauper just like you staying here awhile back. He said he was a paperer by trade, so that's what I got instead of payment: he papered that screen.

No one can say we don't get our share of paupers here!"

77

「うーん。良い仕事をしている。

腕のいい表具師だな。一文無しは腕がいい。

よし。これに絵を描こう」

「だめですよ。白地ならいくらかでも売れるで

しょうが、絵を描いてしまったら売れないよ」

「心配するな。必ず白地より高く売れる絵を

描いてやる。水を汲んでこい」

"Well, well. The man did an excellent job. A master paperer, I'd say. But then, leave it to paupers to do things properly. All right. I'll paint your painting on that screen."

"Oh no you won't. As long as it's white and blank I stand a chance of selling that thing. No one wants to buy a bad painting by a drunken *e-kaki*!"

"Not to worry. I promise you my work will only increase the value. Fetch me some water."

男は、衝立の前に座ります。無心で墨を磨り

まして、しばらく考えていたと思いますと、

衝立一面に、一気に何かを描きました。

「どうだ。これでよい」

「なんですか？　これは。なんだかよくわから

ないんですが」

「わからぬか。これは雀だ」

「あ、そう言われてみれば雀だ」

「では、預けておく。わしが帰ってくる

まで、誰にも売るでないぞ。

さらばじゃ」

The young man sits in front of the paper screen and quietly mixes his ink. He ponders for some time, then suddenly splashes the surface of the screen with a flurry of brush strokes.

"Finished! How do you like it?"

"What is it? What's it supposed to be?"

"Can't you see? Sparrows."

"Oh! Now that you say it, yes, those are sparrows all right. Very lifelike."

"I'll leave this masterpiece with you for now, Zembei. But you must promise not to sell it to anyone before I return. Farewell."

81

かわいそうなのは善兵衛さんで、その晩は女房にさんざ嫌味を言われまして、寝てしまいます。翌朝、太陽が昇り始めた早朝でございます。二階でゴソゴソと物音がしますので、夕べ、虫でも締め込んでしまったのかと思って二階へあがり、雨戸を開けてみますと、チュンチュン、チュンチュン、バタバタバタと、部屋の中から空へ雀が飛び立ちます。あれ？　雀は、どこから…

と、ふと、そばに置いてある衝立を見ますと、なんとっ！絵に描いたはずの雀がいません。しばらくしますと、表でチュンチュン、餌をついばんでいた雀が、またザーと帰って来て、衝立の中、ストンと元の絵に戻ります。

82

Poor Zembei gets to bed that night only after a nasty tongue-lashing

from his wife.

The next morning, with the sun just beginning to rise,

he awakes to a fluttering sound coming from upstairs.

Thinking some sort of insect must have

got trapped up there during the night, he climbs the stairs, walks into

the first room, and opens the shutters.

Chirp cheep fluttery flap! What's that flying out into the morning sky? Sparrows?

How did sparrows get in the room? As he's wondering this, Zembei's eyes fall

on the partition screen, and his jaw drops. The white paper is completely

blank. The painted sparrows are gone!

Moments later, *chirp cheep fluttery flap*, the sparrows return from hunting their

breakfast. They fly in through the open shutter, straight to the blank screen,

and—*pop! pop! pop!*—assume their places in the painting as before.

善兵衛さん、ビックリしまして、

「おい！ おい！ 大変だ！ 大変だ！」

と階段を転がり下りて、寝ている女房を

起こします。

Zembei is gobsmacked. He half-tumbles down the stairs and wakes his wife.

"Oi! Oi! You won't believe this!"

翌日も、また翌日も、おなじことが起こります。

だんだんと、これが評判になってまいりまして、連日、押すな押すなの

泊まり客で、もう大変です。

「泊めて欲しいんだけど。雀の飛ぶとこ、見たいの」

「もうだめです。当分いっぱいです」

「廊下の隅でいいからさ」

「廊下も全部、半年先までいっぱいです」

「お前さん、階段の上から三段目なら、来週ひとつ空いてるよ」

と、そんな具合で、夫婦はへとへとです。

The sparrows pop out of the painting and fly the next day as well, and the day after that.

As word of this miracle spreads, people begin clamoring to witness it, and soon the little inn is overflowing with guests.

"I'd like a room, please. I've got to see those sparrows fly."

"Sorry, but we're booked solid for the foreseeable future."

"I'll sleep in a corner of the hallway. Anywhere's fine."

"All the hallway space is booked too, for the next six months."

"Hang on, old man. We do have an vacancy on the staircase next week. Third step from the top."

Business is so good that Zembei and his wife are running themselves ragged.

89

そんな騒ぎが、とうとう小田原のお殿様、大久保加賀守様のお耳に入ります。

「余もその雀を見てみたい」

All this commotion eventually comes to the attention of the Lord of Odawara,

Ohkubo Kaga no Kami.

"I desire to see these sparrows for myself."

91

というわけで、お殿様が相模屋へやってまいります。

飛び立った雀をご覧になり、衝立に戻ってきた雀もご覧になり、

「亭主、この衝立、余が千両で買おう」

「千、千両でございますか？　ははっ、ありがたき幸せではございますが、カクカク

シカジカで、これは預かりものでして、勝手にお売りするわけにはまいりません」

「そうか。善兵衛、そちは義理堅い男だの。ならば余も、その絵師が帰るのを待とう」

「ははー」

というわけで千両の値が付きました。

No sooner desired than done. His Lordship is escorted to the Sagami-ya.

There he witnesses both the flight of the sparrows and their return to the screen.

"Innkeeper, I'll pay you a thousand *ryō* for this partition screen."

"A th— th— a thousand *ryō*? Oh, my. Oh, thank you, Your Lordship. I'm truly honored by the offer, but yadda yadda blah blah blah, and I'm afraid I'm not in a position to sell that painting without permission from the artist."

"I see. Zembei, you're a man of your word, and I repect that. Very well, then, I too shall await the return of the artist."

"Thank you, Your Lordship."

And so the price of the painted screen is set at a staggering thousand *ryō*.

「お前さん、だから言っただろ？　どこか見どこ

ろがある人だねって」

「うそをつけ。お前は、ちょいビリのひょろっピー

だって言ってたろう」

「千両で売れたら百両ぐらいはいただけるかし

らね。この家、建て直そうね」

夫婦は楽しく、そんな相談をしております。

"Didn't I tell you, old man, that there was something special about that guest of ours?"

"You lie. 'Slippety rippety trippety strippety,' is what you said."

"If the screen sells for a thousand *ryō*, maybe we could keep a hundred or so for ourselves, right? We could rebuild the Sagami-ya!"

しばらくした、ある日のことでございます。

相模屋の表に、人品卑しからぬ老人が、

ひとりの供を連れてまいりました。

「ご主人、飛び立つ雀の衝立がある宿と

いうのは、こちらかな？」

「へい。手前どもでございます」

「ちと、拝見したいのじゃが」

「へい。どうぞどうぞ。お泊まりは

いっぱいでございますが、

飛び立たない昼間でございましたら、

ごゆっくりご覧いただけます」

Zembei and his wife are discussing the situation one day, when a respectable-looking elderly gentleman and his manservant appear at the entrance. "Innkeeper. Is this the place where sparrows pop out of a painted screen?"

"Yes, sir. At your service."

"I'd like to have a look at that screen."

"Do come in, sir. We have no vacancies at the moment, but most of our guests are out during the afternoon, when the sparrows don't fly. If you'll just follow me ... Here it is. Please feel free to study it at your leisure."

97

老人は、衝立の前へ座り、しばらくじっと

見ておりましたが・・・。

98

The old gentleman sits before the screen
and stares at it for some time.

やがて悲しそうな顔をして、

「ご主人。残念じゃが、この雀はもうすぐ死ぬぞ」

「えっ！ 本当でございますか？ 絵に描いたものが死ぬので？」

「絵に描いたものでも飛び回るほどのものじゃ。このままでは疲れて死ぬのじゃ」

「ど、どうすればよろしいので？」

「わしが、死なぬようにしてやろう。止まり木を描いてやろう」

「だめですよ。この雀には千両の値段が付いていますので、変なことすると

お殿様に怒られます」

「心配するな。必ず雀だけより高く売れる絵を描いてやる。

水を汲んでこい」

なんだか以前に聞いたような言葉だなと思いながら、

善兵衛さんは水を汲んでまいります。

Then he turns to Zembei with a mournful expression.

"Innkeeper. I'm sorry to tell you this, but these sparrows will soon be dead."

"What? Is that even possible? Can things in a painting die?"

"If they can fly, they can die. And these are bound to expire of sheer exhaustion before long."

"But, but ... What to do?"

"I can help. I too am an *e-kaki*. I'll just paint them a place to rest."

"Don't you dare, sir! Lord Ohkubo has offered a thousand *ryō* for this screen! He'd be furious!"

"Not to worry. I promise you my work will only increase the value. Fetch me some water."

Zembei totters off, thinking he's heard those words somewhere before, and returns with water for the inkstone.

老人は、衝立の余白に、なにやら網の目のような

ものを描きあげました。

「な、なんでございます。これは？」

「わからぬか。鳥かごじゃ」

「ははあ、そう言われれば、そのような・・・」

「では、ごめん」

老人は、そそくさと帰ってしまいます。

The elderly gentleman mixes his ink and then proceeds to cover a blank space on the screen with crisscrossing brush strokes.

"What's that supposed to be?"

"Can't you see? It's a *kago*. A cage for the birds."

"Ah. Yes, of course. A *kago*. I see it now ..."

"Very well, then. My work here is done. If you'll excuse me."

And with no further ado, the elderly *e-kaki* departs.

翌日、いつものように善兵衛さんが、大勢の見物客が待つなか、雨戸を開けますと、バタバタと飛び立った雀がすぐに帰ってきて、スーと、一旦、鳥かごの中で留まってしまいました。

それがまた評判になり、またまた大久保のお殿様がやってまいりました。

鳥かごで休んでいる雀を見て、「亭主。二千両で買うぞ」

ついに、二千両という値段が付いてしまい、夫婦は夜も眠れません。

The next morning, Zembei is opening the rain shutters before an expectant mob, as always. As always, the sparrows pop out flapping and fluttering, but this time they're quick to return and land on the perches inside the cage to rest. This of course causes a new sensation. And before you know it, here comes the Lord of Odawara again.

Seeing the sparrows at rest on their perches, he makes a declaration.

"Innkeeper. I will now pay you TWO thousand *ryō* for this painting."

And just like that, the price of the screen has doubled. Neither Zembei nor his wife gets much sleep that night.

そんなある日、相模屋の前に立ったのが、あの絵師です。

「善兵衛、久しぶりじゃな。衝立の雀は元気か?」

あの時と打って変わって、見違えるような立派ないでたちでございます。

「先生! お待ち申しあげておりましたわ!」

女房は、大喜びでございます。

善兵衛さんは、これまでのいきさつを絵師に話します。

「何? 老人がかごを描いたと? どれ、早く見せてくれ」

106

Then, on a day much like many others before it, whom do we find standing in front of the Sagami-ya but the original artist.

"Zembei, it's been awhile. How are the sparrows getting on?"

His clothes and general appearance are now so elegant as to render him nearly unrecognizable.

"Sensei!" The wife is beside herself with excitement. "We've been waiting for your return!"

Zembei, for his part, calmly explains everything that has happened.

"What's that you say? An old man painted a cage for the birds? Show me at once!"

絵師は衝立の前へきちんと座り、しばらくじっと 見て

おりましたが、やがて、ハラハラと涙を流し、

「父上。お懐かしゅうございます。親不孝をお許しくだ

さいませ」

「え！　あのご老人は、お父様だったのですか？

やはり、上には上がありますな。

でも、どうして親不孝を詫びるのですか？」

The artist is ushered quickly upstairs. He falls to his knees in front of the screen and stares at it wordlessly. Soon tears are streaming down his face.

"Father! Forgive me for my long absence, and for bringing this shame upon you!"

"What? That old *e-kaki* who painted the *kago* was your father? Well, well. Even the best have their betters, I guess. He's a real master. But why do you say you've brought shame upon him?"

「うむ。老いた親を
『かごかき』にしてしもうた」

"Don't you see, Zembei? I've turned my beloved elderly father into ... a kago-kaki!"

ぬけ雀・オチのあとさき

ぬけ雀は、ずいぶん古いお話です。その起源が関西なのか関東なのかも、作者が

誰かなのかも、今はもう定かではないようです。この話の解説などをググってみると、

もともと、オチは『二つ蝶々曲輪日記』という浄瑠璃の中から生まれたということです

から、上方で生まれた公算が高いようでもあります。『二つ蝶々曲輪日記』は長いお

話ですが、遊女が駕籠に乗ると、その駕籠屋が、生き別れた父親だった・・・という

ような部分がこのオチの源流のようです。人形浄瑠璃は江戸時代初期に上方で生

まれた芸能で、今では想像もできませんが、明治初年頃まで、その鑑賞や習い事が、

庶民の娯楽の大きなウエイトを占めていたようで、この話が成立した時代も、浄瑠

璃のストーリーや名せりふを誰もが知っていた時代＝江戸末期か明治初期（?）

ということになります。そうでないとオチで皆が笑えませんものね。

時代は変わり、話は残ります。今では、浄瑠璃に関係なく、親を「籠描き→駕籠かき」

112

にしてしまったと落とす演者が主流です。いわゆる、大切な親を下賤（げせん）な仕事をさせてしまった。という論理です。そのために雲助（くもすけ）＝街道筋の悪質な駕籠屋の話をマクラでしたりして、理解を求めることが多いようです。ま、オチはともかく、この話の圧巻は、絵に描いたスズメが本物になって飛ぶという、ハリーポッターのようなファンタジーに、人々が驚き、動き出すところです。この落語を面白く聴くには、演者が、主人公、そのお父上、宿屋の主人、おかみさん、お殿様など、登場人物のキャラをいかにうまく立てるかがキモかもしれません。絵本のほうでは、聴衆のイメージに助けてもらえませんから、絵に描いたスズメをどう飛ばそうか、というところが苦心のしどころです。いかがですか？　あなたのイメージにそれほどかけ離れないで、スズメは飛んでいますか？

A WORD ON "POP-OUT SPARROWS"

The *ochi* or punch line in "Pop-Out Sparrows" is an elaborate and untranslatable pun. Homonyms are plentiful in Japanese and provide a basis for endless wordplay. *Kago* can mean "palanquin," but it can also mean "cage," as in "bird cage." *Kaki* can mean "bearer" but also

"painter." An *e-kaki* is a "picture-painter," and one who paints bird cages might conceivably be called a *kago-kaki*. But a *kago-kaki*, written with different characters, is a "palanquin bearer"—which would be a brutal and horribly undignified job for one's elderly father.

落語と観客・賛

舞台の真ん中へ、きもの姿で、ひとりで出てきて、座布団に座って、扇子と手ぬぐいだ
けを使って、話をする。何度も聴いてよく知っているストーリーなのに、観客は笑う。落
語というのは、実に不思議な芸能です。聴く側も、初心者のうちはなんだかよくわから
ないのですが、十年二十年と聴きこめば聴きこむほど、その面白さ、深さがわかってき
ます。衣裳や舞台装置の無いシンプルな見映えなので、そのぶん演じる人の個性や
オリジナリティが出やすいのでしょうか？　同じ噺でも演じる人によって、面白さがぜ
んぜん違うのは、少し落語を聴いたことのある人ならよく感じることです。落語はキャ
ラクターの芸なのですね。

また、聴く側は、シンプルな見映えだけに自身のアタマの中で想像をふくらませやすい
のでしょうか？　そういう意味では、落語は、演じる人と聴く人、舞台と観客の共同作
業のような芸能であるといえます。それだけに舞台と観客との距離が最も近い芸能
であると思います。事実なのか伝説なのかわかりませんが、古今亭志ん生が酒に酔

って舞台で寝てしまったことがあって、驚いた楽屋の若い衆が起こそうとして出てくると、観客から「いいから寝かせておいてやりな」という声が掛かって、寝ている志ん生を皆で見て、クスクス笑っているという、そんなエピソードもあるぐらいです。

落語通の人は、言います。「やっぱり志ん生だ、志ん朝だ、円生だ、彦六だ、小さんだね」。関西人も言います。「落語は米朝やで。いやいや松鶴ですわ。枝雀はよかった。天才吉朝」。

亡くなった人でも、耳に残っており、音源や映像があり、現代人は、時を超えて大勢の名人と一緒に落語の世界に浸れます。しかし、しかしながら、落語はやっぱり舞台と観客、ライブの芸能です。今、生きて、高座で輝いている人々を、足を運んで体験して、しっかり見届けたいものです。落語は生きて、今の時代を呼吸しています。すばらしい落語家が次々と出てきています、現代も。お名前は控えさせていただきますが。

THE HEART OF RAKUGO

Offstage someone plucks a shamisen, accompanied by taiko drum and flute. The performer enters wearing a dapper kimono and takes his place on a cushion in the center of an otherwise empty stage. He bows deeply as we in the audience applaud. Straightening up, he greets us warmly and eases into a humorous anecdote about some aspect of daily life, one we can all relate to. Before we know it, we're laughing. When the anecdote concludes, the performer segues into the main story, which might last anywhere from ten minutes to the better part of an hour.

Without ever leaving the cushion he's kneeling upon, the performer narrates the story, mimes the action, and portrays all the characters, giving each a distinctive voice, posture, facial expression, and personality. His only props are a folding fan and a hand towel. The closed fan becomes a pipe, a dagger, chopsticks, or a writing brush; unfolded, it's a tray, a sake bottle, an umbrella, a broom. The hand towel might undergo similar transformations, turning before our eyes into a book, a wallet, an inkstone, or a fish. The studied precision with which the artist manipulates these imagined objects lends them a reality that helps us suspend disbelief. We become immersed in the action, visualizing the setting and scenery and laughing at or with the eccentric characters and their often absurd predicaments. The performance ends with the *ochi* (literally "the drop"), the final punch line and resolution, and we laugh and applaud as the storyteller bows again and silently exits the stage.

This, of course, is rakugo.

As with most traditional Japanese arts, the framework and techniques of rakugo storytelling have been passed down through the generations via sensei-disciple relationships. It takes years of dedicated training to become a full-fledged *rakugo-ka,* and the disciple must memorize dozens if not hundreds of tales, some very old and some relatively new. The two stories we're offering here are classics. Both have been part of the rakugo repertoire since the Edo period and are still delighting audiences today. A good story has a timeless, universal appeal and begs to be transmitted, but linguistic and cultural differences often present obstacles. Our hope is that by distilling the stories to their essence and pairing them with these luminous illustrations, we can help point the way to the true heart of rakugo.

絵：はやかわ ひろただ（早川 博唯）

現役時代はグラフィックデザイナー、イラストレーターとして活躍し、傘寿に手が届くこの頃は、描きたいものを描く自分自身の絵画に没頭。元気で忙しく楽しい日々を送っている昭和15年生まれ。タイトなスケジュールを超スピードでこなした本書の絵は、愛用のコンピュータを駆使して生まれる。道具は時代とともに進んでも、人を癒す画風は、本人のキャラから生まれる生来のオリジナリティ。

編：もりた はじめ（森田 一）

コピーライターはじめ文章に関する仕事でキャリア約50年。最近は弔辞原稿や追悼文の仕事がふえて自身の年齢を感じている。この仕事、舞台で聴く落語のふくらみが、なかなか文字の上ではむずかしく、悶々としてすすまぬ日々を、落語会へ行きつつ過ごした。最後は、絵本は絵本、別物としての完成度を自分に言い聞かせてアップ。尻を叩く編集者がいて、なんとか無事にゴール。

英訳：ラルフ・マッカーシー （Ralph McCarthy）

日本の小説などの英訳を、何十年も続けている。ユーモアのある作品が特に好きで、太宰治の「お伽草子」、北杜夫の「どくとるマンボウ航海記」、村上龍の「昭和歌謡大全集」などの文学作品や、赤塚不二夫のマンガ「天才バカボン」など、いろいろなジャンルの笑える作品に挑戦できたことはラッキーだった。落語集をいつかは訳してみたいなあと、ずっと前から考えていたので、今回は、とても楽しく味わいながら翻訳できた。

装丁デザイン：かたおか のぶよ（片岡 伸代）

英語で読んでも面白い！ 日本の笑い話

らくご絵巻

2020年1月6日　第1版第1刷発行

編者　もりた　はじめ
絵　　はやかわ　ひろただ
訳者　ラルフ・マッカーシー

発行者　株式会社 新泉社
　　　　東京都文京区本郷 2−5−12
　　　　電話 03(3815)1662
　　　　Fax 03(3815)1422

印刷・製本　株式会社 東京印書館
©Hajime Morita & Hirotada Hayakawa
2020 Printed in Japan
ISBN 978-4-7877-1927-0 C0076